The Alchemy of Love: To Love A Muse

Vonta Moffett

BookLeaf Publishing

India | USA | UK

Presentation by *BookLeaf Publishing*

Web: www.bookleafpub.com

E-mail: info@bookleafpub.com

ISBN: 9789363304772

First edition 2024

To Mom, for believing in me and demonstrating the boundless depths of love. To my children, who reminded me of its protective embrace. To my Ancestors, the roots I'm honored to water.

To love ... a muse.

Love, A song Without Words

A Song Without Words
You are the perfect melody,
A frequency that lifts my spirit,
The only background music that stirs my soul to
dance.
Your essence is a symphony of crystal bowls,
Each note of your voice undresses my
imperfections,
Revealing the rawness within me.

Sections
Like the wind, you gently bend around every
curve of my introspection,
Shedding light on hidden motives, drawing out
confessions
I'm too proud to speak.
I was used to hiding from the world,
But then there was you—
You could sweep me away with force, but you
don't.
You could manipulate and coerce, but you
won't.

I Whimper

You are the nostalgic sound of my mother
calling me in for dinner at 6 p.m.,
The memory of the good times,
When I raced the streetlights home.
You are my grandmother's hands anointing me
with holy oil before bed,
The soft, moist kiss on my forehead.
You are the feeling of staying home from school
on a weekday,
The anticipation of the weekend on a Friday.
You're the thrill of payday when the money hits
my account,
A lifeline when the world counted me out.
Your energy always brings good thoughts.

Distance
You've always known the way to my heart,
Without needing directions.
My soul wandered, lost and in need of
guidance—
That's where you stepped in,
Stripping away parts of me that no longer
served,
Casting them to the four winds.
You offered me up to the Earth's altar,
Where I received your blessing to be more,
Never less.

Silence

Even from afar, you heal me,
Though we journey in different directions,
We've never truly been apart.
In finding myself,
I found you too.
You bridged the gap between my Higher Self
and my personal biases,
Healing the dissonance in my mind.
I learned to observe my silence—
The highest form of love I've ever known.
An intimacy I craved,
A soft touch,
A gentle kiss,
The caress of my hair,
A resonance that awakened my inner witness.

A Testimony
You carry my every tear to triumph,
You are a gift,
My very own present.
A lesson,
My soul holds candid photos of us,
No proof of our connection,
Yet in my soul, I trust in you.

I'm Safe
You give me permission to take up space,
No masks, no façades,
No need to save face.

You offer a patience so steady,
I'd risk it all,
And as much as I hate to admit it,
I'd come running if only you'd call.

You don't demand a false humility from me,
You let me be bold,
Let me be brave—
A bird soaring through the cool blue sky,
Finally free from its scorched iron cage.
I rage with a new beginning,
A fresh chapter,
A blank page.

Because of you,
I sharpen my pencil,
Ready to write my own story,
No longer tracing the lines of life's stencils,
But carving out my own principles.

Love saved me.

Beauty For Ashes

To trade beauty for ashes
Some wouldn't dare—
Perfection gleams like fragile glass,
Too pristine, too delicate to bear.
They chase reflections, flawless and clear,
But beneath the surface, something stirs, a silent
fear.
Some long for honesty, yet the truth is a
sharp-edged blade,
And sometimes, a single lie feels warmer than a
thousand truths laid bare.
We bandage our wounds with deceptions,
Hiding scars that pulse with a quiet ache,
And drift through life like lily pads on still
waters,
Floating gently, careful not to reveal the tangled
roots below.

To trade beauty for ashes
Would it shatter you?
For the ashes speak of pain endured,
Of despair that clings like smoke in the corners
of the soul.
To trade beauty for ashes—it doesn't seem fair,

But what if the ashes carry the strength to rise
anew,
A story etched in the soot of survival?

Beauty for ashes
Or is it the other way around?
Is there beauty in the hope scattered like dust in
the wind,
As we scatter the ashes of a loved one upon the
earth?
Are they just ashes, or do they still hold the
essence
Of a life once lived, of a love that lingers,
A memory that leaves a trace like a whispered
song?
Our minds dwell in that place,
Where their spirit sings in the heart,
Like a caged bird, yearning to soar,
Yet bound by the weight of loss, unable to break
free.

Does it count?

A smile from a stranger,
A child's innocent laughter,
A cool place in the shade from the sun's
relentless heat,
As sweat traces a path from brow to cheek,
A warm embrace in a world that feels cold.

Does any of it count?
Would you trade beauty for ashes,
Or is it the ashes that make one beautiful?
Could you rise, like a phoenix from the flames,
If you had never been burned to the ground?

To trade beauty for ashes
Some wouldn't dare—
Perfection demands too great a price,
But in the ashes, perhaps,
There's a beauty more true,
A beauty that whispers of resilience,
Of strength born from the fire.

The Weight Of Unspoken Love

Is love still love even if it isn't mutual?
Do I rob love of its full splendor
When your heart doesn't echo the same song as
mine?
Do I close love's eyes to the truth,
When I choose to overlook your indifference?
Is love still love, even when it's unrequited?
Love, in its purest form, asks for nothing—
It demands no return, or does it?
All it offers is a heart wide open,
Ready to nurture, to be present,
But is love truly safe without boundaries?
Can it survive the weight of expectations and the
longing to be met halfway?
Does love ache for reciprocity,
Or is it content to simply exist?

Is this love a world I've built alone,
A place where only I dwell,
With feelings that dance unseen by others?
Have I created a universe
Where my emotions are the stars,
Bright and burning, yet invisible to everyone but
me?

This doesn't feel safe—
To love deeply, yet remain silent,
To feel so much, yet never speak of it.
Is love a solitary journey,
An experience that lives within me,
Or is it something more?
Can it truly be called love
If it never reaches beyond my heart,
If it never finds a way to touch yours?
It's like standing face to face with it,
Yet never being able to take in its reflection.

I can't bear the thought of never holding you,
Never knowing the warmth of moments we'd
weave together.
I've tried everything to escape the pain
Of loving you alone, in a dream that feels so
real—
A love I'm not sure exists outside the walls of
my own heart.

Does love really do this to a person—
Make them question, make them ache like this?
I bared my soul to you, laid it all out,
But somehow, I missed the mark—
My words, they stumbled, they fell short,
They couldn't grasp the depth of what I hold for
you.

And these feelings, they just hang in the air,
Unable to close the distance that separates us.
If I'm never satisfied in love until I feel us
together,
I'm terrified I'll stay trapped in this obsession.
Yes, I can't deny it:
I am infatuated with you, utterly consumed.
I am all of these things, completely and without
shame.
Every part of me is tied up in you.
And still, even if I never get to call you mine,
I'd remain this way—
Even if the love I carry for you
Is the love you share with someone else.

Because as much as I'm infatuated and
obsessed,
All I want is for you to be happy, to feel safe,
To know the kind of love I hold for you,
Even if it's not with me.

So maybe love really does come without
expectations.
If this is the love destined for me,
Then even in its unrequited form,
It's still love, and it's still mine
Because through this, I've discovered—
That love, even when it aches,
Lives fiercely within me.

A Child At Play

Did I dream this into being?
I asked God for love, and suddenly, my truths
were revealed—
The love I sought had been buried deep,
Hidden beneath layers of forgotten innocence,
And a child's voice, once silenced, began to
whisper.

I became restless, like a child yearning for play,
Lost in a world that had grown too serious, too
gray.
The voids within me stretched wide,
Like open fields begging to be explored,
Revealing the thirst of a soul that had long been
ignored,
A song unsung, a dream unchased.

As the tides shifted and the storm calmed,
I found myself face to face with someone new—
Or perhaps someone old, someone familiar,
A version of myself I had left behind.

Who is she? This girl with eyes full of wonder,
Her desires different, her dreams untouched by
time,

Her world filled with magic, her laughter
unrestrained.
She emerged, unrestricted, after all these years,
Her voice like the wind through the trees,
Whispering secrets only she and I could know.

I once thought love was gentle, a soft embrace,
But she showed me it was wild and free,
A dance in the rain, a leap into the unknown.
In knowing her, I realized I had lived not as
myself,
But as the shadow others cast over me,
Hiding her light, dimming her spark.

How do I make up for all the years I kept her
hidden?
How do I heal the wounds I inflicted by denying
her joy,
By stifling her giggles and curbing her curiosity?
I embraced the lies, wearing them like a
costume,
When all she wanted was to run barefoot in the
grass,
To paint the sky with her dreams,
To live unafraid of the colors within her.

Love, I found, is as startling as the screech of
chalk on a board,

A jolt to the senses, a reminder of what I had
lost.
I was exposed, never having clothed myself in
love,
My life barren, for I had not nurtured the seeds
She had planted long ago in the fertile soil of my
heart.

I rose to every challenge for others,
My life a constant giving, without a moment to
pause,
Without a moment to play.
I silenced her to protect her,
But in doing so, I became her greatest adversary,
The one who locked her away.

I thought I was shielding her,
But I made her stand on the sidelines as our life
passed by,
And now, as the signs of youth begin to fade,
I panic, fearing I've lost her forever.
I didn't cherish her corny jokes, her obnoxious
laughter,
Her giddy and goofy spirit—
I locked her away because I feared the world's
judgment,
But when I asked for love, it was she who
emerged,

Hoping that in loving her, I'd learn to love
myself.

I owe her an apology,
For the time I wasted, for the joy I denied,
For the moments we could have danced and
laughed,
For the adventures we could have taken.
I tell her the sun is setting soon,
But in her quirky way, she reminds me—
"We still have brighter days ahead."

Perhaps she's right.
It was fear that led the way,
But today, she tells me,
Is the day we let love have its way.
We won't worry about yesterday;
We'll live for today,
And no matter how old we get,
She'll always be the same age,
A child at heart,
Ready to play.

The Light To My Shadow

In Your Light, I See My Shadow

The sight of you stirs me deeply,
Like an artist captivated by the canvas,
I draw you close, as close as breath,
Yet I flee.

I flee from you,
Running hard and fast, escaping,
For in your presence, the truth of my life
unfolds—
A life I never knew I yearned to live.

Every glimpse of you is a mirror,
Reflecting the essence of all I am meant to be.
To see you is to see me,
And so, I run from the sight of you.

Yet, your presence weaves through my thoughts,
Intriguing, compelling, an unshakable thread,
I carry you in every heartbeat,
For to carry you is to carry a piece of myself.

In your absence, I find myself drawn,
For beside me is where I feel you belong.

Perhaps this longing is what makes my heart
grow fonder,
Your essence is stitched into the fabric of my
daydreams.

You are my muse, my vision,
A dream manifesting, a guiding star,
When I see you, I see myself,
A reflection that ignites my deepest truths.

Your presence is an awakening,
Is this love or inspiration?
You are a wellspring, flowing endlessly,
Yet you trigger the rawest parts of me.

From a distance, I observe,
I know your actions, for they mirror my own,
You lead me to parts of myself,
I've hidden, repressed, shrouded in shadows.

In your light, I am revealed,
Unable to deceive, to shield my truth,
What I try to hold back pours forth,
Like water breaking free from its confinement.

Your presence demands honesty,
A space where I can no longer hide,
You see me—every flaw, every strength—
And that truth is both haunting and liberating.

You are a beacon in my darkest corners,
A home I yearn for,
Yet, your light triggers me,
For running to you is running to myself.

In seeing you, I confront my hidden self,
You reflect all I am in truth,
And though this realization is powerful and
beautiful,
I am still learning how to embody her.

So I run, and every escape leads me back to you,
For in every encounter, I become more of who I
am,
And that, in turn, triggers me,
Yet, I cherish this awakening.

In your presence, I find my true self,
And that revelation, though challenging,
Is the light that guides me home.

Held By The Words Of Love

I came ready to fight,
Armed with anger, prepared for war,
Ready to unleash every hurt,
To defend myself, to stand tall in the face of
conflict.

But you met me with something I'd never
known—
A love so gentle, it stopped me cold.
I was used to harsh words,
The kind that cut deep, that linger and scar,
Words that force you to build walls,
To brace yourself for the next blow.

I'd learned to harden myself,
To wear my strength like armor,
To always have a retort,
A shield against the pain of verbal attacks.
So when I confronted you,
I was ready for battle,
Prepared to go to any length to prove myself
right.

But you were still.
You met my storm with calm,

Your silence wasn't empty;
It was full of understanding,
A stillness that pierced through the chaos,
That quieted the echoes of past wounds.

You responded with a gentleness
I'd never known,
Your voice like a soft breeze on a summer night,
Soothing, calming,
Your compassion wrapped around me,
Igniting empathy within me,
Making me see the root of my pain,
Even when I couldn't.

Your words didn't wound,
They healed,
They held me like a tender embrace,
A gentle hand on my face before a kiss.
You made my defenses crumble,
My weapons fall to the ground.

I couldn't be angry;
You disarmed me with your kindness,
Your maturity, your willingness to mend
What I was ready to tear apart.
In your presence, I felt safe,
Like a child swaddled in love,
Realizing for the first time

That peace doesn't have to be born from
conflict,
But can simply exist,
A state of being that you invited me into.

Does love require harshness?
A never-ending rite of passage that demands
suffering,
As if every conversation is an initiation
Proving one worthy of compassion?

Does love call us to suffer?
Must we toil the cursed grounds of sabotage,
Hoping to plummet into a shared experience of
entangled emotions?

With you, I toil not.
With you, I suffer not.
For your words diffuse the magnetic pull of
coercion,
Convincing me that love needs no permission,
That love can simply be.

Since then, I've been wrapped in you,
Drawn to your peace,
Longing to be a part of it,
To live in the calm you've shown me,
Where love doesn't have to hurt,
And where I can finally rest.

Let Love Have Its Way

I trust in what we've uncovered,
Or perhaps, what we're on the verge of
unearthing.
It defies words, transcends logic—
The way you've altered the cadence of my heart.
Like a shipwrecked vessel,
Abandoned and entombed beneath the relentless
waves,
You've drawn me into the abyss of your love,
Where tides surge and crash with raw emotion.
If this is what it means to surrender,
Then let me drown in these depths forever.
For in these merciful waters,
I've discovered a sanctuary, a refuge from the
world above.
We drift together in this sea of contrasts,
Burying the darkness of the world in our watery
grave.
If you were ever to turn away,
My breath would falter, my spirit would wither,
For it is your gaze, your love, that breathes life
into me.

I trust in the possibility of what we could
become,

If we let love take the lead.
I once believed love was a distant myth,
A whispered tale, never meant for me.
I wondered what it would feel like,
To be intricately woven into the fabric of
another's soul,
To feel their heartbeat resonating within my
own.

I was deaf to love's whispers,
Oblivious to her tender yet insistent touch.
I sought her in desolate places,
In lands where her voice had never been heard.

But love, she is a force of her own—
Fierce, unrelenting.
When she calls, her voice is a siren's song,
Demanding to be acknowledged.
She speaks a language of truth,
Unwavering in her pursuit of what's real.
She is relentless, never one to be ignored,
And now, wrapped in her embrace,
I understand her call, her language, her truth.

I have found that love has a will of her own,
She's passionate, persistent,
When she calls, she demands to be heard.
She requires honesty, vulnerability,
A willingness to be laid bare.

To capture a love like this,
One must be willing to expose the most delicate
parts of the soul,
To allow the tenderness within to be cradled by
another.

I trust love's ability to guide me,
For it was she who led me to you.
She revealed your face in the quiet of my
dreams,
Whispered your name into the chambers of my
heart.
Love painted your image in the canvas of my
mind,
Calling me toward you with a pull I could not
resist.

Now I stand convinced—
Love has her own agenda.
She summoned me from the familiar,
Guiding me through mountains and valleys,
Through moments of falling and getting lost.
Love was never my aim, never my pursuit,
Yet she insisted, her voice a constant plea,
Her call impossible to ignore.

This love, our love, is guiding us toward our
north star.
The spirit of love has aligned our hearts,

She has played the role of the oracle,
The role of the judge,
Cloaking herself in strength and honor,
Shielding me from a life devoid of her presence.

She has summoned me to answer her call.
But if I let love have her way, will I be safe?
Will she shelter me from the tempests of
heartbreak?
Even if not, I've learned this—
Love's true purpose is to be experienced,
Even if it isn't destined to last.
For love, like the seasons, is ever-changing,
Yet constant in her desire to be felt.
Her goal has always been to gift me her essence,
To let me taste the sweetness of her presence
through you.
She never demanded perfection, only a willing
heart.

So, I will let love have her way.
For love has brought you to me,
And though the future remains uncertain,
I will cherish this moment, this shared
experience.
For love's greatest gift is the time we have,
And the memory of loving you will forever be
mine.

Mine For Eternity

To know we share the same breath of air,
To know you're here, that you're aware,
Brings comfort to my weary soul,
In this vast world, you make me whole.
Though miles may lie between our lands,
I feel your touch, I sense your hands,
Guiding me through life's unknown,
Reminding me I'm not alone.

If lifetimes stretch beyond this one,
I hope we meet when all's begun.
Even if our paths are brief,
A glance, a touch, would bring relief.
Perhaps you'll be the one who rings
The bell that marks my daily things.
Or maybe you'll be the friend I find,
With love that's true, and hearts aligned.
In every life, no matter who,
I'll recognize the soul that's you.

Suppose this love, so deep, so true,
Is meant to shape and see me through.
It makes me brave, it makes me strong,
To face the world, to right the wrong.
But will you join me on this quest,

Or must I walk alone, at best?
My thoughts of you, they never cease,
They rob me of my daily peace.

Yet through it all, I'd gladly bear
Another life, just to share
The warmth that you bring to my heart,
In every life, we'll never part.
If you're a tree, I'll know your roots,
If you're a cloud, your misted suits.
If you're a dog, I'll know your bark,
I'll find you in the light, the dark.

For you and I, we're meant to be,
In every life, through eternity.
Our love, a thread that never breaks,
No matter what each lifetime takes.
In every form, in every place,
I'll seek you out, I'll know your face.
And love you as I do today,
In every life, come what may.

Will You Walk With Me?

Though our journeys are meant to be lived on
our own,
Would you choose to walk with me, where the
seeds of love are sown?
Your path is yours, and mine is mine to take,
But together, we can venture, for each other's
sake.

Can I join you on the quest to find your truth,
As I peel back the layers of my own soul's
youth?
Let's create a space, honest and bare,
Where faults and wrongdoings are laid out with
care.

Meet me here, where judgment won't reside,
I'll encourage you, with love as my guide.
No act of yours could turn my heart away,
For I see the light in you, growing day by day.

Can I walk beside you, through the doors you'll
face,
As you evolve into your intended grace?
I know you'll stumble, and you'll find your way,

Through the nights of doubt and the brightest
day.

Will you do the same for me, as I will for you,
Holding space for all the dreams we pursue?
My love for you is innocent and pure,
Even if we're not lovers, my love will endure.

If you find another to share your life,
I'll love them too, with no trace of strife,
For they are a part of the one I adore,
An extension of you, whom I cherish evermore.

I can't predict how our paths will twist,
But I promise to be there, through fog and mist.
Your mess, to me, is a beautiful sight,
I've never loved someone with such pure delight.

You are adorned with my love, it's true,
My spirit has chosen and favored you.
The best part is, I know you feel the same,
There's nothing within me that calls out your
name in vain.

I'm open to you in ways I've never known,
Willing to walk with you, where love has grown.
To be your shelter, your comfort, your guide,
With no desire to possess, only to stand by your
side.

I'll never steer you wrong, nor lead you astray,
I want what's best for you, in every way.
I'm willing to walk with you, through life's vast sea,
Not demanding my way, but supporting yours and me.

So, will you walk with me, as I will with you?
Through all of life's journeys, both the old and the new?
I'm willing to do life with you, hand in hand,
Supporting the unique experiences we each have planned.

I'm willing to walk with you, will you walk with me?
Together we'll journey, where love is free.

When Love Departs

When true love departs, it doesn't leave a void.
Its presence lingers, like a warm embrace that
never fully fades, a constant reminder of the
legacy it leaves behind.

When true love departs, it leaves no questions
unanswered, no cards unturned. It gave fully of
itself while it was here, leaving behind a deep
well of compassion, with waters so deep, you
can still sip from them.

I remember when love danced—how it moved
gracefully through our lives, twirling us into
moments of pure joy. I remember how love
protected me, shielding me from harm, wrapping
me in a sense of safety that nothing else could
provide. I remember when love spoke up on my
behalf, lending its strength when my own voice
would shake and falter. I remember love, your
love, our love—the love we shared.

When true love departs, every memory is
cemented in the heart, each one a vivid portrait
of every shared moment. Its legacy pulls you
back into the fullness of every experience, where
it lives on, peaceful and unbothered by time.

I remember how love wouldn't rest until it was sure I was okay, how it would call to check on me, making sure I felt seen, felt heard. I remember how love consoled me when I cried, holding me in those dark moments, bringing light where there was none. I remember love laughing, its sound filling the room with warmth. I remember love visiting me, its presence like a breath of fresh air on a heavy day. I remember love encouraging me, whispering words of hope and strength when I needed them most. I remember how love kept me steady, even when the world around me wavered. This love, your love, our love—this is the love I shall remember, and it shall not depart.

When true love departs, it leaves you with a knowing—that you were truly loved, deeply and beautifully. It fills you with thankfulness, a quiet pride in having been loved in such a way, even if that love is never to be experienced again in the same form. There's a pride in saying, "I was once loved."

When true love departs, it doesn't take you with it. Instead, it leaves a piece of itself behind, offering strength to weather any storm, to walk through any valley, to climb the highest of peaks. Even in its absence, love lifts you up, guiding you through the most challenging of times.

When true love departs, it doesn't leave you seeking to fill the deep voids within. Instead, it takes its final resting place in those voids, leaving you complete, filled to the brim with its essence. In its time here, it only ever filled you up, and in its departure, you find that there's still enough left over to keep going.

So when you find true love and lose it, know that true love is never truly lost. It can never be erased. True love protects by exposing you to what it is, making sure you never go without it again. You'll never accept the false forms of love in its place, for you'll always know the real thing.

When true love departs, you'll find that it still remains. It transforms into the driving force of your life, extending to you its grace. It becomes a part of you, carrying you forward, guiding your steps.

When true love departs, it makes you its final resting place. To have loved, to have seen love's face—it leaves itself behind, a gift of grace to carry you through.

Love is never lost. It comes back again, in the rising of the sun, in the light of the moon, in the comfort found in tears.

Love is never lost.

So when this love departs, I'll cherish the remnants it leaves behind, knowing that all we've shared, I shall inherit as fully mine.

When this love departs, I won't mourn or grieve in vain, for knowing that I've been loved so greatly works as the balm to soothe the pain.

You have gone on, but with me, and in me, your love resides. To know I've been loved so deeply is one of my greatest forms of pride.

The space for our love still exists, and in that space, I can meet you there, to experience it all again.

Thank you for a love that departs yet still mends.

I love you.

Loves Quest

I'll search for you in realms beyond what the eye can see,
In spaces where time and reality don't confine love,
Where your essence exists unbound and eternal.

I'll find you in the last light of the sun as it sinks between the mountains,
A warmth that lingers, even as the day fades into night,
A golden hue that soothes the earth and comforts my soul.

I'll seek you in the gentle breeze that wraps around me,
In the subtle touch of the wind that whispers your presence,
A reminder that you're always near, even in the quietest moments.

I'll gaze upon the moon as it moves through its phases,
Waiting patiently for its fullness, knowing that in its light,

I'll find traces of you, a reflection of your
steady, enduring love.

In the fields of flowers swaying freely in the
breeze,
I'll see your beauty mirrored in their graceful
dance,
And hear your voice in the most beautiful of
harmonies,
Where your voice will always be the richest.

In the ocean's tide as it kisses the rocky shore,
I'll find you in every wave, in every crest,
Seeing the reflection of your love in the rhythm
of the sea.

I'll seek you in all things peaceful and serene,
In life's simplest, most treasured moments,
Where gentle winds and towering peaks become
the landscape of my longing.

I'll discover you in the melodies that touch my
soul,
In the notes of a song that stir my spirit,
Your love turning the ordinary into something
extraordinary.

You are the color in my world,

The presence that transforms the mundane into
something beautiful,
In you, I see life in a new light, where even the
darkest moments hold a certain beauty.

In your presence, I find my safe space,
A sweet escape where all things going wrong
fade to black,
And in your beauty, I find rest.

In my dreams, I'll search for the reality of your
existence,
Tracing every detail of your presence as I reach
out to feel you,
Hoping to bridge the gap between what is
imagined and what is real.

Even in my deepest wounds, in the times when
my spirit falters,
I'll search for you, knowing that your love is
there to heal and renew,
For your embrace is what brings me back to life.

So, I will look for you in every moment, in
every breath,
In every leaf, in every breeze that crosses my
path,
My quest to find you is endless, spanning time
and space,

For your love fills the distance between us and
colors my world in ways I never imagined.

In every corner of existence, vast and small,
In the quiet spaces where life unfolds,
I ground myself in you, quenching my longing
for home,
And cherish the beauty you bring to my life,
For you are the light that guides my way, the
presence that makes every day beautiful.

Warfare Of Love

I once found solace in the quiet embrace of
solitude, a sanctuary I built with my own hands,
where every corner was arranged to my liking.
My heart was a fortress, its gates closed tight,
fortified against the weight of others' needs,
content with the self-love I nurtured in its
stillness. The simplicity of my solitude was a
rare gem, a peace unmarred by the demands of
affection.

But then you entered my life, like a sunrise
breaking through the night. The walls around my
heart, once unyielding and solid, began to
crumble like ancient ruins in the face of your
warmth. Solitude's song, once a solo melody,
transformed into a harmonious duet, each note
longing for your presence. The yearning to walk
alone dissolved, replaced by a deep-seated desire
to journey alongside you, to follow where your
path may lead.

Take me with you, I implore, not out of
necessity, but because where you are is where
my soul feels complete. I seek not just a place

beside you, but a shared existence, where your essence becomes my guiding star.

Take me with you, no matter how distant the horizons. The trek to be by your side is a pilgrimage of the heart, a journey I choose with unwavering devotion. I have come to understand that love is not just a feeling but a mantle of responsibility, and I am ready to carry that burden for you. I hold myself to a higher standard, recognizing that what I bring into your world must reflect the beauty you deserve. Walking beside you is not merely a wish but a destiny that has redefined my very purpose.

I am prepared to shoulder your burdens, to share in your struggles, to ensure you never face the shadows of loneliness. Take me with you, for I will be your steadfast companion through every tempest. Even if the gales of life rage against us, I would brave the fiercest storms to find you and bring you back to our haven. I am committed to being accountable for my actions, always mindful of their impact on you, as if you were a part of me even when you are not physically present.

Even when impatience, like a beast with gnashing teeth, seeks to rear its ugly head and snarl at the edges of my composure, I will step forward, undaunted. I will wrestle this feral beast in your honor, bearing its savage rage with a heart full of resolve. I will not allow the snarls of my inner turmoil to encroach upon the serenity you deserve. I will battle this inner tempest so you may never feel rushed or anxious in my presence, holding you in the calm of my unwavering support.

When my tongue, a weapon of sharp edges, seeks to lash out like a blade dipped in the bitterness of vinegar, I will stifle its venomous edge. I will command it into silence, shackle it with the chains of respect and honor, and redirect its fury into words that cradle you in softness and love. The acid of my frustration will be purged, leaving only the balm of affection. I will fight the shadowy specters within me that threaten to mar the warmth of my words. You deserve not to be cut by my harshness but to be enveloped by the gentle embrace of my expression.

When my ego, pricked and provoked, seeks to withdraw into a cold and frozen passivity, turning its aggression inward and denying the warmth of my affection towards you, I will call it to center. I will hold it accountable, reminding

it of the deep wells of love I harbor for you. I
will guide it back to the essence of my
adoration, urging it to transform from a chilling
force into a source of comfort. Instead of
inflicting harm, it will find you a blanket of
tenderness to shield you from its coldness,
wrapping you in the warmth of my unwavering
devotion.

There's no need to fear this love I have for you.
Yes, I am imperfect, but I am ready to defend
you from the treacheries of the world and the
inner demons that threaten our love. I am
prepared to wage a relentless war within myself,
engaging in a fierce battle against the darker
elements of my nature so that the nobler aspects
will emerge victorious for you. I am willing to
lay to rest who I once was, to obliterate the
shadows of my past, so that I may rise anew and
dwell in the radiant glory of our shared love. So
take me with you.

The agony of this struggle is a crucible I
willingly endure. It is a pain I accept with open
arms, knowing that each battle fought within
myself is a shield to protect you from the
wounds I might inflict. My demons are fierce
and relentless, but I face them head-on, for your
peace of mind and your comfort are worth every

sacrifice. I will confront my inner darkness, wrestle with my own fears and insecurities, to ensure that the light of my love shines clearly and brightly, unblemished by my own shadows.

So take me with you. I have prepared my heart for this voyage, beyond mere words and gestures. I have carved out a sanctuary within myself, a haven where you can reside in tranquility and affection. I have adorned it with patience, kindness, empathy, and compassion. Here, you will be enveloped in joy, laughter, and steadfast support. This sanctuary bears your name alone, a sacred space no one else can enter. I have polished it, prepared it, and made it ready just for you.

Take me with you, for I have laid the groundwork for a love that can withstand any storm. This inner refuge of mine is strong, a place where you will never feel lost or alone. Love is a duty, love is responsibility, and I am ready to embrace both. I will shield you from the shadows that linger within me, ensuring you feel cherished and secure in the home I've created for us.

Take me with you, and together, we will find our way to a place called home.

Ancestral Love

You fought the good fight, with unyielding
might,
Pressed on through shadows, toward the light.
Your faith was tried in affliction's flame,
Purified like gold, you overcame.

You prayed with fervor, hearts full of grace,
Never losing hope, despite the race.
When Father and Mother left you alone,
The LORD took you up, made you His own.

In the depths of mourning, you found joy anew,
Waiting on God, your strength He renewed.
You turned to Him in every storm,
An ever-present help, steadfast and warm.

Wisdom cloaked in power, you passed it down,
And now as clouds of witnesses, you surround.
Your blood still speaks from fields and ground,
A legacy of strength, profound.

May your redemption continue, bold and true,
What was stolen, return tenfold to you.
May your enemies bow low before,
The descendants you fought for, forevermore.

May your lineage grow in number and might,
Strengthened by the day, empowered by the
night.
May the hand of God oppose all who dare,
To destroy what you built with love and care.

May grace abound for those who bear your
name,
And the fruit of your womb, rise in endless
flame.
Be healed of every wound, every scar,
Rest now in solace, power from afar.

Ase, we say, as we honor your fight,
May you dwell in peace, in eternal light.

2/22/21

In the embrace of my mother's house, wisdom stood tall, a sentinel guiding my every step. It was there, in the warmth of her presence, that I found the answers I had long sought. Her words, like ancient rivers, flowed with the grace of time, carrying the weight of generations past. Each syllable was a gift, a testament to the lineage of strength and insight bestowed upon me by the matriarchal bloodline. In my mother's voice, I discovered the divine favor, mercy, and grace that shaped me, the ability to discern and be wise etched into my very being.

When I sought the love of God, it was in her arms that I found it, cradled in the safety of her embrace, nourished at the source of life itself. Her eyes, windows to a soul that saw beyond the veil of the ordinary, gave me vision when I sought to be seen. In her gaze, I knew I was cherished, known, and understood. The safety I yearned for was nestled in her heart, a fortress where I was always protected.

It was in these moments that I realized how deeply blessed I was by God. The bond we

shared, mother and child, was more than earthly;
it transcended the boundaries of life and death.
Even in her transition, the connection remained
unbroken, a golden thread woven into the fabric
of eternity. In this, I understood that God is
eternal, and so is the love we shared—a
relationship that defies time, a connection that
endures forever.

A Time

I'm not certain this was ever part of God's plan,
But I thank you, truly, for what you gave to me.
You sheltered me in ways that I didn't
understand,
Created a space where I could find and just be.

Though we've grown apart, our paths now
diverge,
You kept me safe, hid me from the world's
ruthless grasp,
Allowing me to shed old skins and emerge,
Discovering facets of myself I never knew I
could clasp.

So I thank you, even as we part and go our
separate ways,
With respect for the journeys we each must now
embrace.
Where you go, I cannot follow, and where I'm
headed, you can't stay,
Here is where our shared path ends, and I accept
this space.

Though I'm unsure if this was ever truly meant
to be,

I believe it served a purpose, a necessary phase.
In the contrast of our time, I learned much about
me,
Revealing who I am and what I am not in so
many ways.

I turn to leave, not wanting to look back in
regret,
To avoid the pain of staying, of making you a
mistake.
I must go now, for staying only deepens the
threat
Of resenting what we were, of being who I can't
fake.

Being with you brought me closer to my core,
Exposing the parts of me I struggled to face.
But I don't like who I am when I'm with you
anymore,
So I choose to depart, to find my own place.

We journeyed together through shadows and
night,
But now it's time for me to walk in the day.
The sun sets on what we had, our time is
complete,
There were highs, lows, and thrills along the
way.

I'm not sure if this was ever meant to be,
Or if what we had was even real.
But I go now, for another journey calls to me,
One that promises to heal, to fulfill.

In a way, we protected each other, placeholders
for growth,
Guardians of the space we needed to evolve.
I hope the paths that await us renew our hearts
both,
That love finds us again, whole and resolved.

May love be pure and true when it finds you,
May it be gentle and kind in all that you do.
We go our separate ways with no bitterness or
scorn,
But with gratitude for what we had, though now
it's worn.

When we look back, we'll see how we held each
other's hand,
How we faced life's demands together, as best
we could.
We go our separate ways, and that's where we
stand,
But what we shared was real, and it will always
be understood.

So I release you to your path, as I walk mine
alone,
Though I'm unsure if we were meant to last, it
was our time, our own.

Love Is Quiet

I've learned to let things be, to stand still in the
flow,
To let the storm rage and simply watch it go.
For it's not the storm itself, but the dust that
settles,
Revealing what remains when the chaos finally
meddles.

I know that whatever is left, after all has been
torn,
Is meant to be there, like the dawn after the
morn.
So I've learned to sit in silence, to embrace the
calm,
To be gentle with myself, to keep from any
harm.

I won't let myself unravel, no matter how fierce
the fight,
For I've learned to enter battles as if victory's
already in sight.
In the end, it's not about the storm, but the peace
that follows,
The strength that remains when we rise from
life's hollows.

Abandonment

Leave me if you must, I do not fear your
departure,
Abandonment holds no power over me, no threat
to my heart.
Reveal your true colors, let them shine as you
walk away,
For I stand unshaken, unprovoked by your desire
to stray.

I will not beg or plead for you to stay,
For love is not something I must chase or sway.
Love comes to me willingly, without condition
or plea,
It does not withhold its good, nor does it bargain
its decree.

If you choose to abandon, it is not love that
departs,
But merely you, with your fleeting heart.
For love remains, steady and true,
Unafraid, unbroken, in everything I do.

The Author Of Life

Here's some advice from a sister you didn't
know,
Sweetheart, listen close, let your wisdom grow.
The world can't love, it's lost in the dark,
A mirror cracked, no true reflection to spark.

Don't seek its approval, don't strive to please,
For the world is tangled in its own disease.
To gain the world but lose your soul,
Would be the price that takes its toll.

The world spins lies, its heart is cold,
It's greedy, selfish, and far too old.
Seasons pass, yet nothing's new,
It won't love itself, so it won't love you.

Don't chase the love that it can't give,
Look within, that's where you'll truly live.
Your light is pure, your truth is strong,
Trust your voice, it won't steer you wrong.

The world will change, it will make you doubt,
But who you are is what life's about.
Don't measure yourself by a shifting scale,
It's a game designed for you to fail.

What's your story? Write it true,
No one else can be you.
If you mess up, turn the page,
Start again, don't disengage.

Keep your pen in hand, write your fate,
Live by love, not by hate.
Hindsight's clear, don't look back in regret,
You did your best, so don't forget.

You may fall, you may cry,
But keep your head held high.
There's a light at the tunnel's end,
You can be broken, yet still mend.

No one's coming to save the day,
But that's okay, you'll find your way.
You've got the strength to carry on,
When it's darkest, you'll see the dawn.

Where to next? Well, that's your choice,
Trust in the power of your own voice.
Keep the faith, if not in God above,
Then in the God within, the light of love.

The world can't guide you, it's lost at sea,
So trust in yourself, let your spirit be free.
Carry on, with a heart so true,
The author of life is none but you.

Romance, The Carcass Of Love

I'm done with being sold the illusion of
romance,
A gilded package, shiny and enticing,
Yet hollow at its core,
A mirage that shimmers just out of reach,
Promising everything but delivering nothing.
Romance is a construct,
A delicate web spun from fantasies and
half-truths,
A way of life that brings more grief than joy,
A storybook of fairytales where I'm always the
damsel,
Waiting to be saved from myself,
But I no longer need saving,
And I refuse to be incomplete without you,
As if my existence is a puzzle missing its final
piece.

Why should I sell myself short,
Chasing after an illusion that vanishes like
smoke,
When the goal is to love others as I love myself?
Why would I place you on a pedestal so high,
That I lose sight of my own worth?

Why should I believe that I must suffer in the
trenches of love,
Just to earn its fickle favor?
I am done with the endless fight,
The ceaseless search,
The yearning that twists my soul into knots,
All for love to make its grand entrance,
When the love I seek already resides within me.

Does it not pulse through my veins?
The desire to be loved,
To be held,
To share in the warmth of companionship?
But to chase love is to scare it away,
To fail to recognize my own reflection in the
mirror.
I am done with the hollow pursuit of romance,
For it is merely the carcass of love,
A shell devoid of its essence,
Unable to embody its true fullness.

Have we not been sold a lie?
So lost in the chase for fantasy,
That the beauty of what's real goes unnoticed?
I'm done with romance,
For I too have been a fool,
Caught up in the glittering ideals,
That align perfectly with my imagination,
But crumble in the harsh light of reality.

To be consumed by romance is to buy into love,
To be a consumer of a packaged deal,
Beautifully wrapped in high hopes and
unrealistic expectations,
A shiny box that leaves me intoxicated,
Fueled by the desire to control how you show
up.

But in doing so, I am left blind,
Unable to see you as you truly are,
Painting you in colors you've never worn,
Clutching a narrative that never existed,
Only to wake up and realize I dreamt it all up.
I am done with romance,
For it has kept me from true love,
Led me to dance with distorted realities,
Spun by those whom romance left hopeless.
For love is so much greater than this construct,
This facade of romance.

I don't want it if I have to dream it up,
I want to be surprised,
To be shocked at how you choose to show up for
me,
If I have to imagine it,
Then I don't want it at all.
Your response to me,
To my energy,
To my essence,

Is the only truth that matters.

So I don't want romance,
If it means holding myself captive,
Chained to something intangible,
Pouring endlessly from a well of affection,
That is never filled in return.
Let the fantasy fade,
Let the illusion dissolve,
For I seek the depth of true love,
Not the shallow waters of romance.

An Open Door

I don't mind holding space for you,
Opening the door and keeping it wide,
For I find pride in being your sanctuary,
A refuge where your worries dissolve like mist
at dawn,
And the weight of judgment vanishes into the
shadows.

I don't mind holding space for you,
To sit with you in the quiet stillness,
As you venture into the depths of wounds that
linger,
Wounds that ache to be forgotten, yet demand to
be felt.
I'll be the silence that wraps around you,
A comforting shroud,
Supporting you as you unravel the knots within,
Offering no words but those spoken by the
warmth of my presence.

For I see your growth as a blossoming tree,
Each branch reaching higher toward the sun,
Your transparency like a clear stream,
Flowing freely, unafraid of what lies beneath.

To witness your elevation is to watch the stars
align,
Illuminating my path with the brilliance of your
transformation.
You are a wonder to behold,
A marvel in the art of becoming,
Brilliant, I'd even say a genius,
In the guise of alchemy,
You transmute worlds effortlessly,
Turning pain into wisdom,
Fear into courage,
Darkness into light.

So I hold space for you affectionately,
Not as a mere bystander,
But as a witness to your unfolding,
As you ascend to heights unknown,
Knowing that in this sacred space,
You are free to be,
Free to explore,
Free to grow without limits.
And I, in turn, am honored,
To stand by your side,
Holding space,
As you transmute the world around you,
And rise in your own radiance.

Freedom Found In Love

When love speaks, it whispers secrets not meant
for the surface,
But dives deep into the hidden realms of the
soul,
Exploring the unfathomable dimensions where
light and shadow intertwine,
Leaving no trace, no imprint, like the softest
breath on a misty morning.
Love has the keen eye of a hawk,
Capable of sensing the subtlest stirrings, the
slightest quiver of the heart,
It moves through us like a gentle wind,
unnoticed but powerful,
Guiding us to places we never knew we needed
to go.

To possess love, to capture it, is to
misunderstand its nature,
For love is not a bird to be caged or a flame to
be contained.
Love, in its true form, demands release,
A relinquishing of control,
A surrender to the wildness that it brings.
To hold love is to let it fly,
To trust in its freedom,

To be vulnerable to the risk it carries,
For in that vulnerability lies the true strength of
love.

To experience love is to embrace its boundless
spirit,
To allow it to roam freely,
Untethered and unburdened by chains of
expectation.
Love, when given the freedom to wander,
Will always find its way back to you,
For in its purity, love knows the path home.
You are safe in love's embrace,
Even when you let it go,
Even when it seems to drift far from sight.
Trust in the goodness of love,
In its gentle hands that protect your heart,
In its watchful eyes that cover you like a soft
blanket,
In its thoughtful nature that always considers
your soul.

Allow love to roam,
To explore the wide-open spaces of your being,
For love, in its truest form,
Has no desire to harm,
No intent to cause pain or ruin.
Love's purpose is to heal,
To build,

To create a sanctuary within you where it can
dwell,
A home where it can return, time and time again.

So, let love walk in its freedom,
Allow it to dance in the breeze,
To touch the stars,
To find its way through the forests of your fears,
And to always return to the warmth of your
embrace.
In love's freedom,
You will find the security you seek,
The peace that comes from knowing
That love, when trusted,
Will never betray you.

www.ingramcontent.com/pod-product-compliance
Lightning Source LLC
Chambersburg PA
CBHW061714130726
47996CB00006B/2301